Flight and Earlier Poems

Flight
and Earlier Poems

Vona Groarke

Wake Forest University Press

This book is for sale only in
North America

First edition, published in 2004

ISBN 1-930630-12-3 (paperback)
ISBN 1-930630-13-1 (cloth)
LC card number 2003112834
Designed by Richard Eckersley
Set in Enschedé Trinité
Printed in the United States of
America

For the best of friends — Conor, Tommy & Eve

Contents

from *Shale*

from *Other People's Houses*

Flight

FROM *Shale*

Shale

What leaves us trembling in an empty house
is not the moon, my moon-eyed lover.
Say instead there was no moon
though for nine nights we stood

on the brow of the hill at midnight
and saw nothing that was not
contained in darkness, in the pier light,
our hands, and our lost house.

Small wonder that we tired of this
and chose instead to follow the road
to the back of the island, and broke
into the lighthouse-keeper's house.

We found the lower windows boarded up
and the doors held fast, but one.
Inside, we followed the drag of light
through empty rooms of magenta and sky blue.

This house has been decided by the sea.
These rooms are stones washed over by waves
and spray from the lighthouse
by which we undress

to kneel under the skylight.
Our hands and lips are smeared with blackberries.
Your skin, my sloe-skinned lover,
never so sweet, your hand so quiet.

The sea is breaking and unbreaking on the pier.
You and I are making love
in the lighthouse-keeper's house,
my moon-eyed, dark-eyed, fire-eyed lover.

What leaves us trembling in an empty room
is not the swell of darkness in our hands,
or the necklace of shale I made for you
that has grown warm between us.

What Becomes the River?

Breathe the clean air of death. The river
has no more strength than a stone.
Is this the same sea or a different sea

that comes a little further on the shore?
Which wave has more potential, greater force
when each wave breaks

and is broken like a stone?
The sound of this is no more
than the river makes when it is still.

If it is ever still.
Everything becomes the river.
The sea held close in the river. The aftermath

of stone is nothing but a proof that this is always
something else. That everything becomes itself
to breathe the clean air of death. The river.

The Riverbed

There is sun in the mirror, my head in the trees.
There is sun in the mirror without me.
I am lying face up on the riverbed.
My lover is swimming above me.

The ribbons he tied in my hair are gone,
gone back to their net in the water.
Instead I have silverweed, speedwell and rue,
where once I had his hands to lie on.

Instead I have silverweed, speedwell and rue,
where once I had his arms beneath me.
His body may come as his body has gone —
and the marl will close over again.

Where are your silverweed, your speedwell now?
They have all gone under the water.
Where is your face in the river now?
Drifting upstream to the moon.

I have walked on the floor of the river with you.
I have walked on the floor of the river.
I would lie on the bed of the river with you.
I will lie on the bed of the river.

Islands

In my house at the edge of the lake
what does not end will not return.
A storm may gather in the stance of trees.
I waited for you. I will sing for you.

When you camc to my house for the second time
I had gathered the leaves of the dark in our room.
I lit a fire and a candle to burn
in every window that faced towards your shore.

Won't you call for me at my house by the lake?
Cedar of Lebanon. Silver Birch.
Won't you take me in your boat to the centre of the lake?
Wych elm. Wych elm.

The Tree House

Because someone has been building piles of branches
in the wood, I have been remembering your hands.
I propose to make a shelter with a roof and walls of twigs
so the close-knit warp and weft will keep us safe.
I am saying that I want you to return
and will show you how by laying down
a bed of leaves and soft pine cones
where I will kiss you so your body feels the sway.

I want you home. I worry when the wind
is getting up. I'm sure it's only a matter of time
before the ragged pine behind the house
buckles and bears down upon the roof
to splay my body with needles
and sweet-scented cones.

For the Unkept House

Fill the bucket with water.
Fill the coffin with stones.
There's a full moon over the river
and there's no going home.

Make a well in the water.
Make a house in the dark.
There's a full moon over the meadow
and there's no going back.

Sweep the stars from the window.
Sweep the dust from the door.
There's a full moon over the kitchen
and there's no going back anymore.

Break off the branches that withered.
Break off the flowers that grow.
There's a full moon over the gatepost
and there's no place to go.

Pick the stones from the meadow.
Pick the weeds from the grave.
There's a full moon over the threshold
and there's no time to leave.

Patronage

Arriving from Bath, they were a strange ménage —
a family thrown together by four marriages,
and having nowhere else to go. Four daughters
older than their new mother, and single still:
their chances harried by a father's debts.

He tinkered with prospects and arrangements of trees,
laid out a town to bear his family name,
devised a railway to cut across the bog,
and so made an impression, and settled down
to oversee a world of prudence, tact, reserve,

and writing books. One daughter worked
at a table made of wood from the estate.
While her sisters stitched bright patterns
in a lace-work plot of pleasantries and chat,
she took a clutch of unstrung characters

and muddy syllables, and set them in a landscape
of her own. In which her father recognised a flaw
and had her slightly shift the view from where
she stood, to take in the symmetry of poplar trees
that secured them from the wilderness beyond

but could not distinguish them, after all,
from a future placed elsewhere;
a time beyond him when their house
becomes a final home for the old,
its rooms converted by nuns to maternity wards.

I was born in the ballroom of Maria Edgeworth's house.
I have tried to imagine the line that takes you
from muslin and moonlight to my mother's screams
and then to me, her last, her unstrung child.
But a room will always cover more than it reveals.

A house is one place trapped in another.
With the windows shut and the doors locked up,
it passed for a place no one would choose to leave.
And when they found their way to a separate life,
something of what they could not leave remained.

I have never returned to Maria Edgeworth's house,
but I've passed behind it on the Longford train
and seen them sitting out in the garden.
I've noticed how they turn towards us as we pass,
how their faces are lost in the shadow of the house.

The Family Photograph

In the window of the drawing-room
there is a rush of white as you pass
in which the figure of your husband is,
for a moment, framed. He is watching you.

His father will come, of course,
and, although you had not planned it,
his beard will offset your lace dress,
and always it will seem that you were friends.

All morning, you had prepared the house
and now you have stepped out
to make sure that everything
is in its proper place: the railings whitened,

fresh gravel on the avenue, the glasshouse
crystal when you stand in the courtyard
expecting the carriage to arrive at any moment.
You are pleased with the day, all month it has been warm.

They say it will be one of the hottest summers
the world has ever known.
Today, your son is one year old.
Later, you will try to recall

how he felt in your arms —
the weight of him, the way he turned to you from sleep,
the exact moment when you knew he would cry
and the photograph be lost.

But it is not lost.
You stand, a well-appointed group
with an air of being pleasantly surprised.
You will come to love this photograph

and will remember how, when he had finished,
you invited the photographer inside
and how, in celebration of the day,
you drank a toast to him, and summer-time.

Insomnia

after Marina Tsvetayeva

Black as the image of the centre of the end, the eye
of darkness that sees only light. I love your vigilance,

the promise of birth, a night that breathes rhythms of release.
And a voice that begins at the end of your song.

So that I have words to bend a river of wind towards your house,
I am only a shell where water will be sounding its own collapse.

But this is a matter of years, of listening too long for what
does not fall in the way of light. Let me become as the end
in a chain of fire — night, like a black sun.

2

And yet another window
to betray their empty rooms of sleep.
Perhaps they sip at a gutted candle rim,
perhaps they sit to draw the darkness in.
Or maybe two lovers whose hands refuse
to break apart the dawn.
Every house has
a window like this.

A window set against the night,
their lives, a shadow against the dust.
Perhaps there is a forest of light.
Perhaps there is one black tree.
The wind will grow faint,
the branches stray like threads,
but in my house, the vigil of leaves is scattered,
only to begin at the edge of things again.

Pray for the wakeful house, friend.
And the window met with light.

Penumbra

Your shoulders, our forgotten loss,
days when nothing happened.
When we would sleep to dream
of unclaimed provinces of light
and wake to evenings divided
by a technique of the dark.
Last days. Penumbra. Evenings.
Hundreds of skies to collapse
in the region of afterwards.
So many fallen suns.
The closing moons.

Even there, you would loosen
the parameters,
untie the grass,
unearth the broken light,
and in its crippled flicker find
the patterns of beginning.
Here. And the borders of excluded space
separate against the dark.
A length of time.
Another silence warps against
the pressure of outside.

If There is a City

If she stands before the walls
set with generations of imperatives,
she sees the evening stretch into a city,
lower tendril stars to streets
that are tangent to the roots of stone.

She must imagine a cornflower field
that will fall to the side
of one remembered sea.
And winter set in the frozen orchards
of her father's house.

If there is a river, she will count
the amber or cinnamon bracelets of her mother
in mosaic light. If there is no river,
she will know the place where the river skin
has snagged on empty passages of clay.

And because of the skin that has spilled
a naked burial on the earth she names it
for a time that had her name, an amulet,
a sacred jewel worn from the moment of source
to the journey's designated end.

Is this the end? The thing that is told
is the journey from chaos to the burning star.
Centuries contained against an arc
of dust or glaze the scorched and jasper
ornaments she breathes into a life.

The absence of a life. The city walls.

Home

I always thought this house would hold us;
what we left would stay here, undisturbed,
except to be explained as stories told
of changes that we made to what we found.

In details like the worn upholstery, a cracked door-frame,
the bathroom wall with all our heights marked in,
I found the proof that something would survive
of years lived here, and that in finding it —

on a Sunday visit, or a Christmas stay —
we might come upon a store of memory
that would remind us, call us to ourselves.

I always thought this house could keep us safe,
as when, running from the car
to the front door, late at night,
I knew it was where darkness could not reach.

The dark can make no difference here.
Our house has been blown open
to a vacant future, bleak as January,

in which no window is lit
against the dust and disregard,
where the only sound is the rooks in the chimney,

and the wind sifted through the hall,
closing, opening the kitchen door.

Enclosure

From Tullamore to Woodlawn, the view
from the train is smeared with recent snow.
In muted fields, a river undermined,
walls and ditches all closed in,
a familiar world has been undone
and worked again into an unknown home.

Your house too will be a part of this.
Not far from where this train will pass
I would find the same enclosure there
beneath which your fields and fences,
two ring-forts, the silver birch,
would still be visible to my accustomed eye
as a blemish, broaching a more perfect view.

How easily I find in this a meaning
that will take in both our lives.
Your house, even now, marooned in darkness,
I would see as a refusal of this simple world
where nothing cannot be overcome,
where difference exists to be a kind of flaw,
briefly noticed, finally resolved.

Rain Bearers

When the others have gone, we row out to the island.
A darkness clots the skyline to the west.
There's been talk that summer will not last.

We stand against the trees for an hour or more
waiting for the evening to dissolve in lake water
and music from an endless barbeque.

The seagulls snag on the water.
The line you trace from them across the lake
ends in a beat of pebbles skimmed against the shore.

The fire in the car park eventually collapses.
By midnight, they are packing up for home.
We watch until the last tail light

stutters behind the woods, and fades away.
You shout out our names to claim possession.
The silence brings a sense of being adrift.

In this first home, we sit together
calling out the colours of the clouds
as amber, pitch, or amethyst.

We cup our hands around them,
passing them between us like small gifts.
You say if anything is easy, it is this.

That seems enough. When I close my eyes
there are shadows where the shapes of cloud began.
Your hand, when you lean to touch me, smells of rain.

FROM *Other People's Houses*

Indoors

It breaks apart as water will not do
when I pull, hard, away from me,
the corners bunched in my two hands
to steer a true and regulated course.

I plunge the needle through and through,
dipping, tacking, coming up again.
The ripple of thread that follows pins,
out of its depth, a shallow hem.

I smooth the waves and calm the folds.
Then, to ensure an even flow,
I cast a line which runs from hook to hook
and pulls the net in overlapping pleats.

Which brings me to the point where I am
hanging a lake, by one shore, in my room,
to swell and billow between the light
and opaque, unruffled dark.

I step in. The room closes round me
and scarcely puckers when I move my limbs.
I step out. The path is darkened where I walk,
my shadow steaming off in all this sun.

House Contents

In the disco of a town hotel
boxes are numbered and packed
according to the condition
of their random artefacts.

Wedding gifts from the '30s,
souvenirs from children's trips,
a gilt-framed oil, an inlaid chair,
cut glass and china (chipped).

Objects without purpose,
details adrift from plot:
the piano and piano stool
for sale in separate lots.

Folderol

I have been walking by the harbour
where I see it's recently sprayed
that *Fred loves Freda,* and *Freda cops Fred.*
Which reminds me of you, and the twenty-four

words for 'nonsense' I wrote on your thighs and back
(the night you came home from her house with some cock-
and-bull story of missed connections and loose ends)
with passion-fruit lipstick and mascara pens.

Including, for the record: blather, drivel, trash,
prattle, palaver, waffle, balderdash, gibberish, shit.
Thinking I had made a point of sorts, but not
so sure when I woke up to find my own flesh

covered with your smudged disgrace
while you, of course, had vanished without trace.

House-bound

The blind holds it in check. As you let it down
it tightens its grip on an evening otherwise unstirred.
What you see is a calculated hour which he is likely
to tie up in a darkened, half-dark upstairs room.

What he brings with him is another world. When,
with your loose fingers, you undo him, then its
refuse, its fog, its chips and cigarettes rub off on you.
You can almost memorize it with your tongue.

He brings you messages. You take him at his word
and once a week allow him in. He thinks of missionaries,
the bond that never breaks. Not that it matters.
It's not company you're keeping, but your hand in.

The skein of darkness in his hands is another story.
He is tightening it all night, so that the stars you keep
initially at bay bear down and perforate your darker sky.
Inside of which you lie, and take it as it comes.

It should mean silence, but it never does. The unused
words thicken in your head, the room, your open door,
the road going out of town. Something like
'Good evening'. 'A great stretch.' 'How do you do?'

You think it is a double bind: on one hand, there's the dark
he lays you in; on the other, there's the chance that he might
mean the world to you. That one day, you may wake alone to
a shift of crumpled fields, a room released to light, an easy life.

The House of Hair

It used to be a house of ill-repute.
She said she still got calls at wayward hours
from gentlemen not looking for a trim.

She was quick and supple and made-up.
The punters liked her, she had good hands
and a braided rope tattoo on her inner arm.

She'd dab her wrists with musk after each one.
It drew the room around her fingertips,
the turn of her breasts, her thighs, her shallow hips.

And I, waiting my turn, would watch them
close their eyes as she'd finish them off
by brushing down the last hairs from each chin.

She cut my hair up short and gave it back
with numbers for two wig-makers in town.
I found it three years later, in a drawer

when it had loosened out and strayed
to fill the bag with soft, dark fur
that didn't smell of me, but of her skin.

The Lighthouse

I heard her tell the story another way.
She set it, not in the village, where
the parish priest was telling the crowd
about light in the darkness
and the dawn of a new age —

she set it in the kitchen of their house,
with three women resting
and the day's work done. She told it
so we would listen for the music
of the room when it was still:

the rustle of the fire in the grate;
the single held note of a teaspoon
from which the knitting needles took their cue;
the steady flutter of the carriage clock
that kept their breath in check.

One of them might sleep and her nodding glasses
snag the firelight and scatter it
around the room to return in the more
familiar shine of cups on the dresser,
copper pans, her sister's wedding-band.

In the village, a crowd of overcoated men
sent up a cheer for progress and prosperity
for all . . .
        And in the length of time
it took to turn a switch and to make light
of their house, three women saw themselves

stranded in a room that was nothing like
their own, with pockmarked walls
and ceiling stains, its cobwebs and its grime:
their house undone and silenced
by the clamour of new light.

The Big House

I took it for another ancient ruin
with gaping windows and the roof all in.
But as we drove up underneath its bulk
I saw that what was darkening our truck
was not the shadow of a burnt-out pile
but a stack of tightly-packed hay-bales
built up like bricks, its façade high
and monumental, latticed to the sky.

Around the Houses

'Oh no,' she said, 'you're wrong. Underwood
never came here. And if someone did

write about the ratio of internal
to external air around the vernacular

houses of Irishtown, Ballinadrum,
I'm sure it could not have been him.

For everyone knows he turned off in Clogher
and never made it this far.'

The Sandcastle

We spent ages making it impregnable and fast,
a crenellated keep complete with flag
and drawbridge, moat and blind portcullis.

And ages later, talking our way past
to gold and silver, torches and intrigues,
dark rumours gaining ground outside the walls.

Holiday Home

Pre-fabricated, four rooms and a view
of haycocks and white horses on the bay.
Deckchairs slumped into the flattened grass
edged with vetch and shards of broken glass.
A bed-settee, a fridge in the living room,
the angelus and tea's old news and *Spam*.
Towels that never dried, togs on the wall,
three swims a day, hair always thick with salt.
Trips to the village for water, milk and gin,
and scampi in the hotel now and then.
Bunk beds, one wardrobe, lino on the floors,
rusted window-locks and swollen doors.
Rough rods for fishing mackerel off the rocks,
the *Naomh Éanna*, watched for, twice a day, for luck.
Last year's novels, dog-eared on the shelf,
late games of whist, gin-rummy, twenty-five.
My father, stepping out to lock the car,
humming lines from one of his four airs:
'Galway Bay'; 'I'll Take You Home Again, Kathleen';
'The Mountains of Mourne'; 'When You Were Sweet Sixteen'.
Us listening inside for notes that swayed and fell
in shadows on the back of Weavers' Hill
behind the house, where these days petered out,
like spray thrown up by neighbours' dipped headlights
or rain astray on bracken, heather, gorse;
the journey back inland behind his hearse,
sand in my sandals, his runners in the boot
with shorts and T-shirts, him in his good suit.

The Slaughterhouse

Some gap in the sidings, a man too few
at the turn into the pens, and they were out,
scattering like buckshot through the cars.
Until a clutch of lads in bloodied aprons
bore down on them with shouts and whirring arms.
Within minutes, they were gathered,
it was done. The lads strayed back to work,
the steel doors closed on the skirl and din,
the driver tidied his gates, and pulled away.

It was chill to the bone. I had been called to come.
I was late, though I didn't know then, not on the journey,
with the plain-chant of the train seeing me home
through towns that came too slowly,
like final words, like beads in her hands;
not when I passed within miles of the house;
not at the station; not as I watched
the flurry of pigs; not when they were bested;
not while they were killed; not when I was driven away.

The Empty House

When we are gone, the house will close over us
as though we'd been swimmers in an unmoved sea.
The cisterns will unruffle, the fridge will wheeze on,
and the shape we made in the bed will pucker out.

The house will replace us with sounds of its own:
the shuffle of pages as we pull the door hard,
the phone ringing out, the occasional clock,
and only the letterbox will break the settled air.

All these shadows from the beech tree in the back
that close on my arm as I reach to turn the key
will swell with a glitter that will take in the room
and, this evening, drain what is left of us away.

Other People's Houses

for Conor

Last night I walked to a house where we
once lived. It's not looking good.
There's been a fire and the roof's caved in.
The garden's scotched with grass and weeds
and most of the windows are through.

The ceiling of the sitting room is upended
on the floor. No trace now of the yellow
couch that was our 'amour prop',
or the stack of romantic novels you had me
stand up on to save your aching back.

Or the radio we lived by in those days,
you with your cricket and creaky plays
on the BBC; me with my news on the
hour, every hour, lest something
outside of us should ever change.

Or the soggy mattress where we sailed
beyond the beyonds and, somehow,
back again to wake each morning
to the blue of our eyes and the three
mile trek for newspapers and milk.

Or the porch where I used to write those
flowery poems before I knew you so well,
halfway between the In- and Outdoors,
where one time, looking two ways at once,
I saw you stranded in both, and thought

I would throw in my lot with yours.
Which is about it. We lived in
other people's houses then. Now,
we have a stake in a place of our own
which keeps us steady and tied.

I want you to know, not that nothing
is lost — even I could not promise
so much — but that something remains,
here, even after so many years:
the starlings are still nesting in the eaves.

And last night as I watched them
their circular orbit put me in mind
of the rhumba you danced with a bumble-bee
right there at the gate, on the day that we left
this house behind us, together and for good.

Outdoors

It happens so easily. We've been watching trees
gather shadow on the wall, on the lookout
for a moment when we might call it a day
and settle for the night. But only our room
is losing ground, while nothing outside is lost.

In the time it takes for him to turn to meet my eye
we have missed it; it has happened without us again.
I give in, put on the light, and watch for him to be
stranded, confronting me from the garden, his back
to me in the kitchen, his eyes, in the glass, on me.

What does it matter that we have made a home
where we can draw the curtains and talk of tomorrow,
if we are thinking of this: the shapes we made in darkness,
our kitchen at sea on the lawn, our table set out
in the branches, our faces marooned in stars?

The Haunted House

Think of rooms threaded by voices. Think of home:
the typewriter chipping away at the small hours;
a stack of ancient newspapers and the scissors
surely blunted by this time. 'Think of home.'

As though you could step in and find them
waiting for you with your tea kept warm.
As though I could keep one hand on the lock
and the other on the handle of the door.

Either way, there's a headless doll that will
never be found under a tree in the yard.
There's a thin voice singing 'I dreamt I dwelt'
and a stream in a ditch where the house dips in

that has my face in it. The time is now,
and I never will step into this house again.

Flight

Along thy glades, a solitary guest,
The hollow-sounding bittern guards its nest;
Amidst thy desert walks the lapwing flies,
And tires their echoes with unvaried cries.
Sunk are thy bowers in shapeless ruin all,
And the long grass o'ertops the mouldering wall;
And, trembling, shrinking from the spoiler's hand,
Far, far away thy children leave the land.

from 'The Deserted Village'
by Oliver Goldsmith

The Verb 'to herringbone'

Something beginning with slightness
and possibly taken from there.
As though unheard of, inauspicious,
the way a pheasant or a wood-pigeon
will find a point of no return, on a lorryless
side-road or on the lee side of an air.
Something begun and veering off at once

as though to double back would be the point of it
and diminution would be a slight recall:
something with an underscore,
though currently unsure how to proceed
or to convince. Like the verb 'to herringbone'
or the air displaced by flight.

Quill

Say one feather is plucked out from that flurry on the board,
dipped for no good reason in the dead bird's blood,
and let drop on something clean to hand, by way of plot —

so that it fixes on a shadow that is not to do with height
because the spine's unbroken and the vane is stiff and squat,
unruffled, like an open book with pages still uncut —

might even that one feather have an inkling of the fate
that will make all of this possible, because flight is not?

An Own Way

A road like any other: early, sheer, littered with unlit yards
and houses with their backs turned, and then no house at all.
A short-cut that she chanced on out of a town that stuttered
on syllables and junctions and estates. She checks her watch
at the shuttered barn and again at the crossroads with the bottle
that hangs by a red rope from a tree. There is only her breath
on the windscreen to remind her that she goes this way alone.

This is how it will happen, she thinks, in such a place as this,
with only these jackdaws to pick at her name and a lambent
aftermath to mark her end. So it occurs, like any other way:
early, sheer, littered with silence and flight. For all she knows,
they are setting out the table even now, while the lighthouse
dims on the oilcloth, and they ask each other again how far
away the town is, and how long it should take her to get home.

Flight

Effortless and uninscribed, the sky
has earthed everything outside
where even bleached flight-lines

are ground as small as the pellucid breastbone
of a golden oriole or wren
between the thumb and palm of my right hand

to a powder that settles on this:
the point at which two rumours coalesce,
one to do with vision, one with voice.

One minute, it's ruse and colour,
the next, wingspan and whir.
And who's to say just what occurs

when something loses the run
of itself and slips airborne
and downwind into the auburn

undertone of flight. And so, away
from the calligraphy of swallows
on a page of cloud; tern prints on snow

that almost lead somewhere,
but then break off and stutter
underground, or into breathless air.

Closer to hand, there is the slight
precision of the black and white
and its close score and countercut

that becomes what happens here,
between these squat characters
and a thinning fiction keen to aspire

to a sequence of hard words laid
one on the other and back again
like a schoolgirl's braid,

chaotic and restrained; that cannot
be taken in hand; that's here now, but
working up to clearing itself out;

soon to be thin air; nothing to write
home about; an advancing quiet
that throws this into shadow underneath

where, by way of leavetaking this time,
death, like a moth in a paper lantern,
is rattling in even these lines.

Thistle

'And love ties a woman's mind
looser than with ropes of hay.'
—Andrew Marvell, 'Ametas and Thestylis Making Hay Ropes'

It's hard to get away from hay these days,
what with the warm weather and the news
from home. Last year the price was high,
but this year they'll be giving it away.
The fields are stitched and cross-stitched
with its high-wire bales: the smell is such
I find I'm driving with all the windows down
past rows of unstooped and bare-chested men

which pass for a vision of the pastoral round here.
As I may have done to some different car
and another driver crossing our farm-gate once
when July was in heat. My father paid fifty pence
to the two of us for a full day's work—
me to the weeding, my brother to his fork—
but the men had their serious labour. I was the only girl
in a field bristling with hands, a stray in the herd.

My brother worked with them from the middle out
and I picked the edges clean of thistles and ragwort.
I was for hedges, he for height,
already eyeing up the stacks he'd make of it
in the barn, thinking taller with each trailer
from the fields, until he was pressed against the rafters
and had to stoop as I did, row on row,
in my small, careful and remunerated way.

That meadow gave good hay year in, year out.
We'd use what was needed, sell what was not
and see it off on the back of another man's jeep
to farms with too little grass, too many weeds.
Long after my hands healed over the thistle barbs
and the summer was closeted in cardigans and scarves,
that hay was holding out awhile over those lean
weeks while the weather righted and the year filled in.

Until I found myself head-high to the heat of a day,
singing again to the frogs and the stiffening hay,
small words in a small tune to kill the hours
that skirted their rough talk and fine acres.
What we saved there was unpoisonous and sweet
and it came again as the same meadow, the same weeds,
the same hay I last made when I was twelve,
the same ragwort I discarded, that still thrives.

The Way It Goes

Choose one version. Turn it. Let it go. See how it spins,
what it fastens, what it sheds. You could call it a thread
that leads you or a tie that binds, but this is a landscape
wasted by the fervour of clean lines. You were one for
happenstance and the story that belied its ordained end.
And where in all that tangle of fresh starts and dead stops
could I find a place where I might rightfully begin?

Side-lit corridors, six-panelled doors, copper pans
and ancestors in rows like chimney stacks and poplar trees
that hide a nest of cottages laid in grass that grows too tall
and is strewn with pig-tailed daughters and knock-kneed sons
who face the world with a different, side-long view
in which the furrows and fencing-posts head one way,
and the ditches and the open road another.

The wall of the yard is darned with stones from the house.
Someone says there was a family of them, though what
became of them is no-man's guess. Now and then, something
turns up: a horseshoe or the base of a crockery pot. And once,
a slate with a fretwork of lines that may have been a name
or half a name—Fox or Cox, maybe. A hard sound to finish with,
for certain, though the start of it is something we can't say.

There must have been other houses that fell in on themselves
this way. I think of you and your inside-out voice going over
and over a brittle, third-hand past. That was towards the end.
'There was no one in the corridors, the windows were shut up.'
And later, dragged outside by the scruff of another incident,
how they walked and passed no one but the remaining
animals which did not avert their eyes. How many roads now?

How many eyes? In those days nothing came of anything,
the wind whipped their heels and words, it was every man
for himself and the billy-cans' rattling made herds of them.
And night no mercy either, dropping past the point
where breath was cupped and handed round, where
there was nothing but a steady count that took you
to dawn's luckless hour and stories of another night survived.

April. An excess of lilac turned them round towards home. May
brought rhubarb so their breath soured over intermittent fire.
June. A memory, their mouths were stopped with it. Then
the summer fruits came in, and nothing for it but sweetness,
an aftertaste of briar. When the boy died, they couldn't bury him,
but left him ashen with soil and recompense, though
his mouth and fingers were smeared with a likeness of blood.

You favoured stories that end in silent death and someone
obvious to blame. You left me your grandmother's ruby ring
and the tune of a song she used to sing. We cleared your house
before the sale (it barely filled a skip), and I took cuttings
from the garden that have never really thrived. So it goes.
My sister got the furniture. With my share, I bought a plot
by the sea where I grow poppies and cornflowers and weeds.

I lived with them, though it was never mine, unless you count
the tree he gave me, or the stones I lodged in the wall. Once
you picked an egg up from the grass to say it was the same blue
as his eyes. Enough. The flags are yellow, the rushes green,
the years have made them grow. I threw soil from their grave
on the rosebush by the door. It yields a good and heavy scent
which you would say is dark and rank and given to excess.

I have known the give of fruit with its too-easy flow.
I have walked those roads. If I can double back to my hearth,
my bed and my intentions, I mean it as no ordinary return.
What can I say? I wake to a taste of dreams I don't recognize.
I call your name. Or I follow the path of dog-roses and
wayfarer's friend that are always here, that pay me no heed,
or that bend as I pass, and straighten as soon as I'm gone.

Sunflowers

Foot soldiers in a long-drawn-out campaign, slumped
under orders, heedless of the stakes,
when news of broken ranks comes dripping through.

Come another way: passengers herded on a platform.
See how they shoulder each other, bearing up, streaming
towards what unsoiled air there is beyond their grasp.

In the height of the here and now, summer presses on us
spoils of chocolate, coffee, wine. The boot is crammed,
the children are a half-inch taller, gilded, sound asleep.

Maize

for Tommy

The Faber Castells ripen in your hand.
You've been drawing since breakfast:
sky after sky, face after face, but something
in yours says they're not quite right.

Every fresh character is dipped
in your range of skins —
beige, primrose, lemon, sand —
and still found wanting.

You finally settle on maize
but not before almost a sheaf
of paper has been scorched
with a repertoire of possible flesh.

The pages rustle into place. I'm watching you
and every irreproachable, off-tone face
is your own in the back of our first white Polo
when one Sunday landed you wide-eyed at the door.

Your head then was marooned in arrival
like our papier-mâché moon.
See how you've given it petals,
wings, hair I can run my hand through

the way the wind cross-hatches
an open field where corn is sweetening
in its cornsilk skin; where yellow
falters, gold begins to maize.

Tonight of Yesterday

for Eve

The evening slips you into it, has kept a place for you
and those wildwood limbs that have already settled on
the morning. The words you have for it are flyblown now
as the dandelion you'll whistle tomorrow into a lighter air.
But, tonight, your sleep will be as round as your mouth,
berried with the story of sunlight finally run to ground.
You are all about tomorrow. The moon has your name
memorized: the curl of your back; your face, an open book.

Oranges

Say you approach   your house in winter
home from work   or in from the shops.
The light is on   in your living room
and the blind   still up. So you stop
to watch the shape   your family makes
against your home.   Your lover reaches
to a high shelf.   He could see you
if he turned his   head your way.
Your daughter   reads some words
you did not write.   Your son juggles
two oranges   or is in flight
between corners   of the room.
Your life shines   without you.
The keys blaze   in your palm.

Family

My mother has gone and bought herself a piglet
because none of us comes to visit anymore.
George has good manners and is clean in his ways:
he is courtly, thoughtful, easy to amuse.
He goes to Mass with her, and sits sweetly
while she trots up to receive. He doesn't stray.
She has made a cot for him in the kitchen
where he turns in on our old clothes cut to size.

One Sunday I call on the way to somewhere else.
She props him up beside me in the high chair
and he fixes me with those dreary dark blue eyes.
When I tell him I'm glad he's there when I can't be,
he answers 'thank you' in a voice too like my own,
then bids me sit and make myself at home.

The End of the Line

Your entry, Last name, First name, *should be here*
at a point beyond the one where you set out,
convinced of a purposeful journey, though
assuming its title uncertain and the subject too big
to pin down. Which leaves a name, and even that
open to inference and a thousand prior claims.

One of which could even be your own. So, see
where it gets you, with time on your hands
and a fancy for tripping on what you might have done.
Take it as read. There's a regiment of enlisted facts
that goes on and on without you, although you
never really joined and have yet to be called up.

But a space exists where everything that might have been
can still be summoned up and slotted in,
so even a syllable might be enough to catch
you out, or your name be a commonplace
where books you never thought to write abound
and where, you find, that *The History of Syphilis*

was the issue of your hand, or that, despite yourself,
you'd done a job on *Paraguayan Folk Dance*
or *Aubergines for All*. So much for memory.
So much for your input. All those hours
of clock-watching and far-fetched plans
that somehow stretched beyond days

you stopped counting and a plot that never came
to very much. But might have been wrapped up
in a couple of lines that say it all, or headings
that run you to earth in the full stop that comes
hard on the last word for you. Another dead end.
Go back. Re-enter the sequence of your derring-do

downriver, where your (as yet) unharnessed life
begs to be a category of its own, slipped in between
America and a miracle, between a haiku and a hairdo
or, better yet, betwixt an undine and undying love.
Home. You've gone as far as you care to go
in that direction. Nothing comes of it. Call up instead

a moment when a scroll of ersatz ancestors,
rattling their corsetry and canes, is filing
past the newborn to authenticate the claim.
Except the cradle's empty and, instead
of your own legend, the words declare,
Your entry, Last name, First name, *should be here.*

Or to Come

'— for the living know that they will die,
but the dead know nothing.' — *Ecclesiastes 9*

There are always unvisited corners
where the only sound is the turn taken by dandelions
or a robin rustling in the aftergrass nearby. Where
a wooden cross tied at the joint bears no name or date
and where what is absolved goes deeper than the darkening
grain where a cursory coat of whitewash has washed off.

The dear bouquets will have sweated a film of rust
inside their plastic domes, and the bare bones
of a handful of wild flowers in a jamjar hold their own.
It could be the churchless graveyard with a stile
at one end and a row of recent yews put down
to mark the high wall off from the estate.

Where graves of couples, and the odd stray child
who died young and will forever pine for crisper
company than theirs to upbraid her elders
with her unused life, go unremarked
under the weight of memorials that are stained
with lichen and damp and generations of disregard.

Or an acre that knows the steady traffic of Sundays'
early Masses and, on holy days, Devotions.
Where the grotto with the kneeling, ashen girl is lit
at night by a halo in the crown
of the blue-robed figure with a bemused face.
The priest switches them on after evening Mass

as he makes the cross from his mutton and bungalow
to his divine estate. On All Souls' Night,
he leads a vigil in which a handful of headscarves
and a single girl give him back the answers
to have them wrapped up in 'Amen'.
The glow of the bulbs keeps them all in thrall

and gives them a look of pitted rhapsody, though
they are only counting beads on a length of chain
and feeling the cold in the far ambitions of their feet.
Inside, the truer candles wither in their bronze clasps.
Tuppence each. One pound would fill the whole of heaven
at Our Lady's feet in the earthy Men's Division.

Where men kneel on their caps and swipe their knees
with them, twice, before the off. Who will herd
out the gap under the gable wall to give the slip
to the crombied visitors and their boxes at the gate.
And PJ in his braces and his stapled trouser hem
who has the news of subsidies and the Bishop's latest whim.

After Mass the graveyard will throb with the saved
who call in on the dead to survey the state
of their prospects and the plot. Their husbands
will toot horns after a decent while, their papers
propped on the dashboard, and the kids in the back
getting anxious for their PlayStations and dinner.

And so they move off and take their noise
and expectations with them, and what remains
will be held in remembrance of those
who could walk with purpose and talk in pairs
and would lie, that night, in symmetry with the ones
whose names and futures they'd been left.

Come Tuesday morning, the caretaker will have
his work cut out with the stray papers and butt ends
blown on from the car park that will press against
the gates and corner stones or be tossed up
by a stray whim of the wind. He will take
to his rounds and his boots will impress the gravel

so there will be a shuffle that follows his progress
and breaks only when he stops to pick the wrapper
of a Ritchies mint from the lee side of a marble corner pier.
He tends the verges on the other days, and knows
the lie of the land and why the grass darkens on one patch
and why nothing will grow in another.

Every now and then he will sit on a headstone
of a small girl's grave, from where the fields are squat
and laid out in their clean straight rows
right down to the bottomless lake
where three Johns will have to drown
before the end of the world. (He knows of two,

though one was JJ who went in after a ewe
and left no family to say for sure
what the letters of his Christian name stood for.)
For the rest of the week, the graves in his patch
are visited by the curious or bereaved.
He knows them, as he knows his care, to see.

By the boy, perhaps, who comes off the bus
a stop too soon to tell whoever will listen
about how quiet the house is and how hard it is
to get up when she isn't there
to call him again and to dampen
down his hair and wave him off.

Or the woman who comes in early
in all weathers with a bag of crumbs that she casts
on her daughter's grave to bring on the birds
that will keep the small girl company and the soil
picked clean for another while when she can't
be there to mind her for herself.

Or the man with amends to be made who spends
too long at the grotto and will not cross
the threshold of the church to say whatever
it is he says over and over to the blue-robed figure
who looks over his head at a sky which she
seems to think may bring her some relief.

Or the girl who says nothing when she comes
once a week, but sits on the kerbstone
and trickles small stones, and lays down
her hand where she thinks his face should be;
who kissed the soil there once, then brushed
her lips more briskly than she wanted.

Or the woman with no flowers for the grave
who brings instead the clamorous prayer
that is her son and daughter
chasing shadows between graves
and calling names that she knows
no one has used for quite some time.

Or the man who reads his name
in stone and finds only strangers;
who fills his pockets with chippings and plastic
petals; who kneels and prays when he is bid;
who runs his index finger over words
that have been occluded and undone.

Another day and he could double as the unknown man
at the edge of the open grave, throwing soil
on the coffin of one he has never met
because the sound of it comforts him
and the tears he sheds on his funeral suit
are as wet and unassailable as theirs.

He'll have scraped the earth of a hundred
burial paths from his well-shone boots.
He'll have eaten the turkey and ham
at a hundred afters, swopped small-talk
about men he never knew, doffed his cap,
and been subdued with priests in every county,

been the wielder of handy umbrellas, handy words,
the giver of cold comfort to relatives
who suppose he is an in-law,
or a far-out cousin, at a comfortable remove.
He is always there, one way or another:
he takes note. He likes the reassurance

and the role. His prize memento is a mirror
which he picked up from where the father
of the little girl had thrown it when it misted
with his hand's heat that he took for her breath
and screamed her back to sudden lidless life.
He tends to bring it with him on his rounds.

Not for him the trembling shoulders
at the side of a filled-in grave;
not for him the reckless offices of grief.
He sees nothing but the ground
beneath his feet and the laden air
that billows with his every heartfelt word.

Leave it to others to see things
as they are and to allow for anything,
either obvious or slight, in the simple facts
of headstones, flowers and graves,
that may just be nothing more or less
than the bare bones of an overriding plot.

Who will slip a foothold, despite themselves,
on the ground they've made their own, and take
themselves out of a landscape that has been closing
on their swansong even yet, like the chippings
of the first stones on the coffin, or the fall and rise
of so many consolations and their rattled notes.

So that all that remains is to lie on and listen
for a sound that a name will not make
where a well fills with purpose, and riddles
through what recent bones seep in;
where a tree is decked with prayer and promises
they'll bear in mind, though it is only a laurel tree

and there are rats in the wellhead
and the family voices grow thin and, then, wear off.
But what of that? Though words are crisp or brittle
and even prayer may be parched from time to time,
the dead know whatever the dead know
and they will have nothing to do with the telling

unless it is an air chanced on a gatepost by the wind
or a chord of water dripping in the well.
There are those who would let every headstone
keep a gap in it. And those who say that names
were meant to escape us; that our ends
should give a slip to all our aims. Who knows?

What happens happens, and the rest is hanging on
for what may come and how it comes to be. What's left
will settle in a place out of their hands where the gravel
will shift in position, where the yew trees will deaden
the wind, where the grass will advance, where the soil
will undress, and the sky will bear down on it all.

gräv

In flight above the tune of a lament for parted friends,
the fingers winnow from the air those notes of upstaged love
and play about the grieving to be done. Both thumbs
hold up to pay their dues: immovable, unmoved.

Half-rings

It begins with lovers
on the verge of an event.
Half-rings and promises;
the hero and the maid
whose lives are not destined
for the common run.

In the sweetest song
he vanishes, returning
after sixteen years
to tell of press-gangs
and a foreign war.
She is married to another,

they are lost.
He does not grieve,
but mournfully besets
her world with fire.
She, in her turn,
takes his life

and makes of it
a token to remind her
that the story is an old one,
the rings not meant for use.

Nouns and Verbs

Between the lighthouse and the vied-for verb
to fix what the beam was doing to the air,
we scattered brilliance with our every move,
two bickering visionaries on the hoof
between dawned-on and unvisited skies,
flights of fancy and our manky shoes,

and came to rest on 'shimmy', 'shoulder', 'segue',
calling it quits, not seeing how the vague
cliff was pinning itself down to a thin line
that we'd have crossed with even one
more unilluminated step, to wimple (indeed)
our own way to the furies underneath

with their ultimate nouns and unwavering calm or,
deeper still, a silence to steal clamour
from adventurous mouths, while nothing occurred
that wasn't spray thrown up by fine words
coming down a-tumble round our ears
like dust; like plucked feathers.

Coming To

for Conor

Like a fist unplunged from the river
and held on high for us to count
until the final drips traipse
from your ring back to the deeps

we wake to this: a first skin
still impressed by dreams that slip
through the eye of daylight
to arrive at ours. And whole days

blanched on the coverlet
where your shoulders round
on promises already spilled
too far and wide for us.

Here's one: the edge of a curtain
lifted by a strand of air so lissome
the day dawns on us all over again.
Another: that it could happen like this

over and over; a last half-hour steeped
in the not-yet-said, and my poring
over it for fear I'd miss a pulse
in your coming to. And still —

everything now is held like breath
between the second last and final
notes of a song turned lightly
to summer and its slipshod overtures.

Which brings me to the sight of you
coming up from the lock, your mouth
streaming, your hair in need of my fingers
and a wide, complicit sunlight on your back.

The way you wake. The way
I am waiting for you.
We could do this all morning.
We could go on and on.

To Be Said

Let's walk the shoreline with it all
to be said and nothing between us but salt.
Let the waves trip on the part of your name
I don't dare. Let the shingle cup your footfall
and the sea-wind straddle the breath you don't use.
We'll hold our tongues. Let you say nothing,
and then, with your voice in my mouth,
I'll say nothing back.

En Route

Even the Foxford rug is black and white
though matted with a wayward heat
that makes your fingers swarm under the cover
in a lapful of your sleek, unsworn intentions.

But all the lies on which we ride
are buckling, like the oyster beds, behind us
and your elver hands are teeming
with their currency and catch.

They surface to fiddle with coins.
I pull in the wrong side of the toll-booth.
You proffer change, say '*Un aller retour*'.
Then we drift into the slipstream, slip away.

The Mooring

'How pointless is the boat that rots on water,'
you write, but I tell you that it comforts me to think of it

steeped in the place it loses twice a day
at the point of what was yours before the breach

that set itself on closing over you or, failing that,
on a boat that cannot slip the knot you tied.

So I could just let it rot or, failing that, could
set myself to find a useful course for it to run.

Such as decking it out in a blaze of candles
fixed in their own wax, and letting it slip

from the mooring away to the deeper draw.
As though you had need of a send-off or,

failing that, some vast heroic death.
I suppose it could flounder in the face

of so much darkness thrown its way. Or,
even yet, might persevere, to be seen by

a stranger on the high road into town
or, failing that, coming the way back.

The Magic Touch

It didn't matter that days would flitter by,
the way you told them: it could have started
anywhere and just as easily slipped our hold
and wandered off without our every word.

The way, once, a fleet of hot-air balloons
sashayed over the beeches, and sailed on
(though that could have been a detail you put in).

Like the self-portrait done in wrapping paper,
or the sand-hill that you posted to me once
to bring — you said — the blue back to my eyes.

Because of all the hiding places, your favourite
was the one between my hands, where you learned
to make the most, I know, of silence and thin air.

You always had the knack of miracles. No one
worked a trick the way you did. But you saw through
the most we made of what we'd amounted to:
limbs; nothing in particular; maybe skin.

Snow in Summer

It was something of nothing; it was nice for a while.
I was learning names that had other names
and how they could work, or be made to.

We took to going places, arriving close to nightfall
and leaving before dawn. We took to being
not easy to pin down. We took to traffic, short-cuts

and cheap rooms. We took chances. We took
off. I had the map and the instinct for direction.
He had a good idea of just how far we'd go.

I'd collect the usages we'd practise later
with the blinds pulled down, trying on
the local accent like a damaged, outsize suit.

It got so that we liked these small pronouncements
and the way we left them after us, as though
they could be found some other time, and made sense of.

One night, drunk on gin and variations, I called
him something which could not have been his name
and I gathered this was one nuance too many.

He called a halt, as though he was all for honesty
and the opposite of sleight of hand, which we,
neither of us, ever could pin down. His name

for me was 'Rosebud', and I came to picture him
with a flat cap and a stoop and far too many metaphors
for me. It was all talk. We cried off when summer did,

tired of asking 'Well, what's that supposed to mean?'
Anyway, the leaves were almost on the turn
and the roses, such as they were, had gone too far.

It was snow in summer. It was love in a mist.
It was what do you call it and what is its name
and how does it go when it comes to be gone?

Veneer

Give me my hand on his neck and his back to my breast,
my heart ruffling his ribs and their flighty charge.
Give me the sea-grass bristles on his shoulder-blades
and his spine, courteous and pliable to my wrist.

His back is a child's drawing of seagulls flocked.
I knuckle the air undone by their windward flight
and draw from their dip and rise my linear breath.

Were he standing, my tongue could graze the whorl
at the base of his neck and leave my hand to plane
the small of his close-grained waist.

Were he lying down, I'd crook in the hollow
of him and, with my index finger, slub the mole
at the breech of his back that rounds on darkness
like a knot in veneer: shallow, intricate, opaque.

The Bower

Arbor vitae — a tree-like appearance seen when
the human cerebellum is cut vertically.
— *Chambers Concise Dictionary*

When it does grow up one has no hesitation in
calling it a tree but it is not so easy to define what
is meant. — Ray Proctor, *Trees of the World*

POPLAR

He's a gossip and he brings it home to her
how big the world is, how small her doings are.
His statements have the ring of consequence,
so she listens and is sparing in response.
He could say anything to her, even her name, and still
sound like small leaves tossed in a summer squall.

WILLOW

We're told the day is promised poor,
but still the weather holds and not even the lake
is bothered by so much impending doom.
The one disturbing factor is the pike

which likes things sour, and so takes on the shore
and its neat symmetry, which he soon sets astir
as he smudges the surface, and ruffles the sand,
and lifts the moored rowboat a fraction higher.

One branch of a weeping-willow skims the surface
and is moved with the lightest of tremors
by the wave. Then the whole tree is suddenly at it,
twittering and jiggling like a nervous horse.

Someone looking from the window pulls her cardigan
tight around her chest and shivers slightly,
as though lifted too, then shrugs to say:
'Well, let it happen, it can do no harm to me.'

Rufus, standing on a flex so the light
dims for a second, offers added proof.
Someone setting down a bucket in the yard
is an echo of more thunder on the hoof.

One of the men decides to light a fire
which will warm them through the worst
of what's to come. 'Best be prepared,'
he tells his woodpile, 'get in first.'

BOX

What I liked about him first off was his height —
five feet four — with a chest like Hercules and hands
like trowels. I'm four foot nine myself and I am tired
of being asked to sit on laps. I want a man
who can look me in the eye while standing up.

He says that I made a man of him with my busy hands,
that I put shape on him, egging him on towards
moves he'd not have made, left to himself. I don't know.
Sometimes I see him when he's perched at his desk.
He looks to me like a bigger man, trimmed back.

ELM

He says that he hardly notices, that I don't look all that different
and, now that the redness is gone and the stitches are out,
you'd think everything was the way it always was. I'm glad
to hear it, but I know it's crap. His tongue says it one way,

but his hands have it another. He hasn't touched me on that side
since the op. Oh, he'll work away at the other right enough,
but he turns his head (who'd blame him) towards the wall. I do
the rest myself, running my finger, for company, round the stump.

YEW

I misunderstood. He was talking about
what went on forever and was hard and dark
and never thought of death, and it so near.

I was seeing graveyards at dusk
with rooks and bats and a full but foggy moon,
while all the time he was talking about me.

COPPER-BEECH

He has taken to pottering and has planted a tree.
He takes long walks. He says no one listens to him
anyway. It's getting so I hate my days off work
and the way that he sours the house with his moods,
so I go into town with Grace, who never asks.

Last Monday, she held up a v-necked blouse
and said it would suit me — I should try it on.
She was looking me hard in the eye and I knew
what she was waiting for, and what it meant.
I came home to cry in my room. He did it again.

I might not need the scarf tomorrow. They're fading,
looking less like the liver-spots on my mother's wrists
and more like the leaves on the sapling
that I see him tending now with his gloves on,
to keep his hands and fingernails from harm.

PLANE

December, and the stand of planes in O'Connell Street
might just as well be lit with crossfire as with these fairy lights.
Xerxes has finished shopping and has left the battlefield
of Clery's with his list ticked off, when he sees it, straddling
the no-man's land between Abbey Street and Lydia.
Crowds mill round him, but he can't take cover or advance.
Which leaves him gazing for another age on the bedecked face
of his beloved and its glow. While to his left, just out
of sight, goes the last bus to Thermopylae, heading south.

EBONY

Madrigal-smooth, with lines that hold their distances
like voices from another room. The broader strains
are breath held against itself for just too long,
while the lighter ones are given to lustre and to sway.

I am holding out for a note to be sounded from
unfathomable ends, when you have something simple
to bestow. Your voice will not give.
Let it use my name against your own,
allow their vowels to darken, to spread out.

WHITETHORN, AND THEN

Plucked like a leaf from a whitethorn hedge
and put down almost at once before the flowers tarnish
or the promise of worse luck can come my way.
Of this, the house and its bright door are innocent
as Sunday evenings or a whitethorn hedge
with all the light flocked into it. Any hour of late.
A kitchen table with plain flour sieved unfairly
so the table's even gleam is done away,
with nothing to show for it but my hands
and their business to do with a white-handed home
or the waiting on for the first slice to be dressed
with cream that will gather itself against the heat,
and turn like small buds to a square of warmth
that comes lately when there's nowhere else to go.
I make a well and count the seconds until
the water fills and the crumbs begin to topple
in the small deep like flecks of whitethorn
strewn on a hedge when there is little else
to see from inside and, anyway, the heat has
blanched the view into something so seemingly
close. Like the twin lambs that will probably buck
my broken playpen in the back of the garage
for what is left of light over Auburn Hill.

Drama

Even the drama of the laburnum tree
backed into the evening sun —
a Roman abundance, a gilded spree —
is as nothing compared to the look
on your face when I directed you to it.

Cities and Flowers

So your city is a garden with its heat in flower,
stiff with outlandish vibrancy and spill.
And your skin rustles like petals on the turn
to wisps of music more fragrant even than blossoms
with their careless overtures. So buildings are laying
slabs of shadow out, workmanlike, the way a tree
could never be, with all that giddy lineage, those airs.

Well, my garden works its allusions to the death,
but the poppies remind me of lipstick, the hydrangeas
of noise. I'm wearing high heels that will stake
me to my place. There are pavements to be set tinkling;
streets that need only breath for them to swell.

En Plein Air

Six weeks on a student exchange in Pont Aven
arranged by friends of my sister's au pair friends
which landed me right in a bristling divorce
and a set of parents fraught and furious.
The village was *gentil*, its views inbuilt
on cornfields and their spontaneous gilt
that came to its own conclusions in the high
ambitions of a couple of cypress boughs.
He'd leave the house at 6 a.m. and come in
at midnight to the bed-settee turned down.
She chain-smoked and took to sleeping late
in a fug of insults I never could translate
while their troublesome daughter had an exchange
of her own with a decorator from Limoges.

Artichokes, *Orangina*, tarte tatin,
a third-hand collection of French reggae bands.
The chic sister up from Paris at weekends,
the lads on mopeds that dropped her home again
in the small hours. Inspector Clouseau on TV,
laughed at by no one in the room but me.
Chantal's friends, bikini-d and sunkissed,
me in a black one-piece with a padded bust
and freckles and my one practised French phrase.
Occasionally, the rows would get too crazed
which were the times I'd light out on my own,
with my phrase book tucked up high under my arm,
calling through the closed doors on my way,
'Maintenant, je vais me promener.'

Cuttings

Today, the outing is to Castle Proud, and we are taking the bus.
Sheila saw it in the paper. It was her idea.
Her grandmother used to work for the Prouds
as a scullery maid for seven years and, never once,

in all that time, she said, did they call her by her real name.
I said they must have called her something
and Sheila said they called her Rosie, because Cook said
that suited her so much better than Pauline.

Sheila's granny told her that Castle Proud
had the nicest flowers of anywhere she'd worked.
The avenues were thick with jasmine
and the lawn had camomile and mint in it that were

invisible, but when you walked over the grass,
the scent your feet released was something else.
We're for the half-ten tour and, afterwards,
we want to walk those gardens and the lawns.

We have canvas hold-alls in our shoulder-bags
and a pair of secateurs. We're gardeners, you see,
Sheila and me. We swop clippings and advice.
We're martyrs to the programmes on TV.

When we get back, we'll have a whole new crop
of cuttings to take root amongst our dahlias and phlox.
I'm hoping for gardenias, and, maybe, fleur-de-lis.
They're quite exotic. You don't get them round here.

Shot Silk

News comes in wisps: the candles flinch
from a fire seen on the hill, torch-light in the wood,
the back door found open again. Rumour streams
up from the town. Maddy's hem needs stitching.

She works between the fire and the roses in the window.
Her face is flushed, her back tingles with cold. Last week,
it was her glove, a tiny rent in the seam that still took hours
to mend. '*Fretwork*,' she thinks, '*is that what this is now?*

'*And what was it this morning when the heart*
of a blush rose came asunder in my hand. News?'
Even now there is business to attend to. She looks up.
Maddy sees another petal tending towards the wood

and a seam of dust is brightened by a flicker of outside.
She could think of a story, one she might shake out
the way the bolt of dusky silk was unfurled on the counter
for her to run her ungloved hand upon. '*Fit for a queen*.'

Here it is now, become a dress, held under by gloves
of skin from an aborted calf which (for all its *tendresse*)
stiffens on her hand. Ashes of roses are spilling at her feet.
The dress will need hanging, but she will leave no mark:

nothing to be quietened or eased into the desultory current
of silk. The petal frets. Someone calls a name out in the hall.
But how would that fit in a story? Or the gloves on the table?
Or the last three stitches, already coming loose?

Imperial Measure

> We have plenty of the best food, all the meals being as good as
> if served in a hotel. The dining-room here is very comfortable.'
> — P H Pearse, the GPO, Easter 1916, in a letter to his mother

The kitchens of the Metropole and Imperial hotels yielded up
to the Irish Republic
their armory of fillet, brisket, flank. Though destined for more
palatable tongues,
it was pressed to service in an Irish stew and served on fine
bone china
with bread that turned to powder in their mouths. Brioche,
artichokes, tomatoes
tasted for the first time: staunch and sweet on Monday, but by
Thursday,
they had overstretched to spill their livid plenitude on the fires
of Sackville Street.

A cow and her two calves were commandeered. One calf was
killed,
its harnessed blood clotting the morning like news that wasn't
welcome
when, eventually, it came. The women managed the blood into
black puddings
washed down with milk from the cow in the yard who smelt
smoke on the wind
and fire on the skin of her calf. Whose fear they took for loss
and fretted with her
until daylight crept between crossfire and the sights of
Marrowbone Lane.

Brownies, Simnel cake, biscuits slumped under royal icing.
Éclairs with their cream
already turned. Crackers, tonnes of them: the floor of Jacobs'
studded with crumbs,
so every footfall was a recoil from a gunshot across town, and
the flakes
a constant needling in mouths already seared by the one drink
— a gross
or two of cooking chocolate, stewed and taken without
sweetener or milk.
Its skin was riven every time the ladle dipped but, just as
quickly, it seized up again.

Nellie Gifford magicked oatmeal and a half-crowned loaf
to make porridge
in a grate in the College of Surgeons where drawings of field
surgery
had spilled from Ypres to drench in wounds the whitewashed
walls
of the lecture hall. When the porridge gave out, there was rice:
a biscuit-tin of it for fourteen men, a ladleful each that scarcely
knocked
the corners off their undiminished appetites; their vast,
undaunted thirst.

The sacks of flour ballasting the garrison gave up their downy
protest under fire.
It might have been a fall of Easter snow sent to muffle the rifles
or to deaden the aim.
Every blow was a flurry that thickened the air of Boland's Mill,
so breath
was ghosted by its own white consequence. The men's clothes
were talced with it,
as though they were newborns, palmed and swathed, their
foreheads kissed,
their grip unclenched, their fists and arms first blessed and,
then, made much of.

The cellars of the Four Courts were intact at the surrender,
    but the hock
had been agitated, the Riesling set astir. For years, the wines
    were sullied
with a leaden aftertaste, although the champagne had as full
    a throat as ever,
and the spirits kept their heady confidence, for all
    the stockpiled bottles
had chimed with every hit, and the calculating scales above
    it all
had had the measure of nothing, or nothing if not smoke,
    and then wildfire.

Here

We should know if we're done for
by the time the news from the outskirts filters through.
Whatever that may mean. It all seems steady enough:
not a whisper out of place in the goings-on. At five,
the buzzer sports its bluster and fools no one.
By nine, the streets are trying on the usual
pock-marked lovers and their flawed rebuffs.
Every doorway opens on a theatre of speculative odds
and only the maudlin and the outraged know the score.
The rest of us trade what allure we can in whatever
episodes we might concoct. While the evening takes
its wide-eyed trumps and moves on to what's possible
elsewhere. Leaving the question of who cares now
for the override of lazy compensations,
or the clutch of the here and now with its glib relief?
Who will take this on, when we already bank upon
the casual distractions of the doomed?
The mountains drag and the roads fill with those who chose
to gamble on the latest, meagre word.
The town reeks of elsewhere and its borrowed lexicon
of how things ought to be. Last week, they found a skull
on a gatepost. Lately, it was a pewter plate on a building site
with the words 'Ye citizens, hold fast' somehow intact.
Then the rose window of the church was smashed
and mailbags were vexed with a shrill, repeated note.
Since that, nothing much. Helicopters at dawn.
My children sleep with their arms above their heads.
The poppies give themselves up to a northerly.
The same rooks throb the rim of the windmill
and branches, like ruptured sails, sear ambitious trees.

Currency

It might have been a groat, a whale tooth or wampum,
the hare that flurried for all it was worth
across the counter of May Deasy's general store,
bobbing between tendered change
and snatches of chat about greyhounds and sows,
between slabs of butter, shoelaces, ham
and the shadow of a raftered violin
that waits on still for the alchemy
of a single correct note;
and was run to ground in the sedge of December,
or found a bolthole in a bottom drawer
to spend itself in darkness —
untallied, unearmarked, free.

White Noise

Lamplight on the paving stones (echoic, gold,
as though the midnight bells from New Year's Eve
still held their own brass wishfulness to heart)
begins to ripple through a crowd on Henry Street,

where hard-pressed eyes are focusing on one yellow voice
and the abstract arc that links Little Denmark Street
with every second before and since that pipped its way
towards history, or news. It aspires to London,

to fall as hail on accents losing the run of themselves;
on a strain of Dame Nellie Melba's aria delivered
to a microphone long since mute; on the time it keeps
with the clamorous sequins of her black wrist-bag;

on a stippled echo faintly falling still with all the other figments
of a world that comes to nothing if not feedback from the crystal
flecks of sound that scatter the riff of masonry, the stiff riposte
of parchment under fire, a backbeat of rifles in popular songs:

'Bye Bye Blackbird'. 'Someone to Watch Over Me'. Inaudible
now if not as snow that faintly falls behind the O's and Mac's
of Dr Hyde and the not-needed daughters of the revolution
who slipped through the button-holes of Miss Rosalind Dowse

to play 'The Maid of Erin' and 'The Hand in the Glove'
to the half-cocked biscuit barrel and a wireless-set
skirted in gingham of green and orange delicate squares.
Loud as fiddles that play on regardless of all that might fall

off the edge of their world, where an eddy of voices is trying
to make contact with them back in Tír na nÓg, pleading
with them to listen, and be warned. Only to be drowned out
once more by dry confessions, static chat and sound advice,

by a Sunday dinner in Ballyhoodeen washed down with peaches,
Neapolitan ice-cream, and a commentary of the final showdown
beween the Caitlín Ní Houlihans and O'Donnell Abús.
And a voice that always knows the score between sequence

and sequins; sects and sex; between Hyde and hide; the dial
and the Dáil; between a murmur and a crowd
proclaiming again to close-knit rooms a dumb-song of stones,
traditional air, the cleared white noise of the Irish Free State.

Breath

See here. The dust that beaded the inside of your cheek
falls still on these letters, on the pages of a book

where someone else's hand will scuff its sleek veneer
and set it skywards, like seagulls astir

on the estuary, cheers from the pitch,
sleet from the Cooleys blown that way, and this.

Look up. Winter skeets the thin skin of the dome
and even the clouds condense the moment

into the here and now of your high mouth,
this flurry of words, or the thought

of what becomes you, what you might yet create.
So yes, let it happen. Let it be you. Breathe.

World Music

Okay. Elvis is driving inland
in a black Morris Minor
and white studded shirt. What else?
He's singing, of course,

a patch-up job on 'Sweet Vale of Avoca'
and 'When they begin...' It's 1974.
He's seen it all. Even today
he's been through Keenagh,

Ballymahon, Tubberclair.
The names are getting longer
and he's flicking butts, like Hansel,
in a trail. He wants out.

But not before his head-to-head
with the Bethlehem Céilí Band
and their full-throttle version of,
of all things, 'Blue Suede Shoes'.

So just when he's coming up to our gate
I'm ready for him with my book and pen.
Nothing surprises Elvis. He throws me
half a smile and a cigarette stub

that I swoop on, almost dropping,
in the process, my crêpe-paper flag
with its red, stapled stripes
and its thirty-two pointless, tinfoil stars.

Pop

It's all love and loss and what was never said
these days, when our radio's jammed between stations
and we oscillate from talk of war to organ fugues
and a spray of pop thrown over night-time hours.
We ghost events, significance and sound, and want
to think this better than a silence we've compiled.

Last week the headset of my Walkman buckled
just as the voice inside aspired to new heights
it never would scale now. So Dusty didn't
make it to the French bits, and those words
(*Ne me quittez pas*) were beached on the other side
of some vague silence, glittering and pristine.

Where they were useful, maybe, to those whose work
it is to gather in our unstruck notes and words
we didn't speak when there was time and breath
to let them go. Whatever had been on the tip
of the tongue, that never slipped; a misremembered
name; a choked-back curse; a promise almost made;

unruffled grace notes; misplaced tunes, and all the
unwritten songs about being young that never got us
anywhere. Like the one I love but can't remember,
getting the words in the chorus all mixed up.
I know it isn't 'live' although I sing it. It's 'leave'.
And it's really not 'forever'. No, it's 'over'.

Acknowledgments

Acknowledgments are due to the editors of the following publications where these poems, or versions of them, have appeared: *Chicago Review, The Dublin Review, The Irish Times, Leviathan Quarterly, Metre, Michigan Quarterly Review, Poetry Ireland Review, PN Review, Poetry Review, ROPES, The Shop, Stand Magazine, Thumbscrew, Tri-Quarterly Review,* and *Verse.*

'The End of the Line' was commissioned by the Millennium Library Information Systems Project. 'White Noise' was commissioned by RTE to mark the seventy-fifth anniversary of Irish broadcasting. '*En Plein Air*' was commissioned to accompany the Ulster Museum art exhibition 'Land of Heart's Desire'.

'The Way It Goes' won the inaugural Strokestown International Poetry Competition in 1999. 'Or to Come' won the *Stand Magazine* International Poetry Competition in 2000. 'Imperial Measure' won the Davoren Hanna Poetry Prize in 2001.

'Tonight of Yesterday' was published in a limited edition series to mark thirty years of Gallery Books.

The author acknowledges receipt of a Bursary in Literature from An Chomhairle Ealaíon / The Arts Council of Ireland in 2001.

Thanks are due to the staff of the Tyrone Guthrie Centre, Annaghmakerrig, where several of these poems were written, and to Dundalk Institute of Technology, whose continued support underwrites this work.

Notes

Page 41 "Around the Houses"

Underwood: A fictional English writer, based on those who visited Ireland during the nineteenth-century and who recorded their impressions of Ireland in the throes of depression and political unrest. Although these visitors penned many of the first-hand accounts of the famine that survive, their writings tended to focus more on social matters of diction, dress, house styles, and drinking rituals than on the historical tragedy unfolding before them. *Irishtown:* a common name for that part of an urban settlement where the Irish were forced to live, and where housing tended to be more cramped and less sanitary than in the grander end of town.

Page 75 *"gräv"*

The title is the phonetic spelling of the musical notation 'grave', indicating a pitch falling, or failing to rise.